Far Better Than Bad

Meredith Larsen

Presentation by *BookLeaf Publishing*

Web: www.bookleafpub.com

E-mail: info@bookleafpub.com

ISBN: 9789358369878

First edition 2023

ACKNOWLEDGEMENT

I am very grateful to have the best support system: Travis, Holly, and Rick. Thank you.

A Whole Hug

In the same way one grabs the clump of hair to
untangle the knots,
To ease the pain;
I have strands attached to my being.
And often, my grasp of those strands, slips.
I lose the tug o' war.
I soak in the ache of missing the very best pieces
of myself.
I wonder when a hug will feel whole again.

Be Prepared

I dream in fragments of situations that have yet
to occur.
I'm not foreseeing any sort of future.
I'm over calculating the potential of my plans,
Of my words,
Of my actions.
I'm sugarcoating the frequency with doubts,
Because it's not only a repetition in my sleep
cycle,
But in many others.
To dream in reality,
To fall forward in moments that could operate as
so,
But more than likely won't.
To bulletproof your waking life with words,
Like a script,
To better the chance of you putting someone in
their place.
In which, places you ahead.
Lucid dreaming with the idea of taking yourself
anywhere you want to go.
But instead you just soak up these mental notes,
Correct responses,
Right answers,
With hopes they won't weigh heavy in your back
pocket.

Provocative Sneak

I've been collecting my time like leaves to a
vine.
Clustered & crowded, it's all gathered in my
mind.
I savor your words like people among lords.
Anxious & waiting, they rush at me in herds.
I retain the negative like a camera's main
objective.
Harsh & narrow, it paints me insensitive
You are what makes me weak like roots
breaking concrete.
Damaging & beautiful, you are full of deceit

Skipping Stones

A skipping stone sitting by a lake,
You're smooth in texture & heavy in weight.
Never to cower or be dismayed
Whether that's a predicament or how you were
made.
Someone picked you up, someone tossed you
away.
Someone lost hope, someone went astray.
But from that pressure came something cruel.
You sustain life, you are no fool.
Like a skipping stone sitting by a lake,
Someone picked you up, someone tossed you
away.
Little do they know you aren't one to be
persuade.
Instead of plummeting, you tread water.
Skipping your little heart out, only stopping to
alter.
You simmer back down, claiming refuge in the
cool.
Surrounded by a new climate, you adapt to new
rules.
Housed amongst plenty.
Cherished by many.
A stone is thrown with the idea of being alone,
But as far as we're concerned,
You are home.

A Moment Of Silence

I saw you standing there with your chin down to
your chest.
I assumed you were contemplating the density of
our planet
Or just staring at a stain on your dress.
How could I suggest any worse than the idea of
you thinking you're second best. Gazing at
yourself or the ground.
Taking a gander at nothing all around.
Absorbed in your doubts, your suspicions.
Adding intensity to your questions, your
decisions.
That's fine, that's more than okay.
I spot your discomfort & find it redeeming, even
swell.
Admiring someone lost in their own submission
I fail to see their magic when they notice my
position.
It's a terrifying realization to find that you've
been caught
Full of daydreams that are adjacent to your own
valid temptations.
Or better yet, that you've been caught tricking
yourself,
Just as you wish to trick others.

That's about when I get the dissatisfying taste of
potential lost.
Eventually I decide to recollect my thoughts.
Then attempt to find a desolate one that's not so
cross.
Don't fret, though, you'll be a memory for a
moment, a memory for a day.
That's at most what I can give to someone.
A moment of silence before walking away.

Outside Of My View

As soon as I began leaving you out of the
conversation
Is when I realized we were through.
You were no longer the punchline.
You weren't even a main course.
You were choice words that I chose to ignore.
Your figure was so mute I felt no remorse.
That is exactly when I knew,
That's when I recognized,
You were no longer special.
You were outside of my view.

I should have ran for my life.

Your lips felt perfect pressed against mine.
Never once did I think
They were not meant to touch.

That feeling outweighed most of my intuition.

Hugging you was like jumping into a pit of
pillows.
I could not picture anyone else
Making me feel as comfy and secure.

Those thoughts devoured my second guesses.

Looking into your eyes when you weren't
engulfed
Was akin to stepping on warm coals;
Cautiously hoping the embers would not ignite.

I should have ran for my life.

Magic Equates To Fate

I am jaded, even slighted,
For life has dealt me quite the hand.
But then I lay next to you,
And I feel I could start again.
I let go of my breath
And settle in for the night.
Though this unknown is chaotic,
Oh, how it gives me life.

I've never had a hand
Touch me with such certainty.
I had yet to feel passion
With little, to no vanity.
Every love song on the radio
Has something I relate to.
Even if it is minute,
Those melodies never fail to sing true.

Damned to be a cliche,
Forced to lose my voice,
Cursed to question love,
Forever doubting my choice.
But then there you are,
Who has brought air to my feathers,
And warmth within knowing

The damage I have weathered.

This could be a week, a month, or even years,
But it wouldn't matter,
Because I have found light
Within your genuine flatter.
Lust is a love.
The latter may hold more weight,
But all stages factor
When magic equates to fate.

A Boy Most Devine

There was a boy, with arched fingers, and
crooked toes.
Whose knees were squared with a tiny nose.
His stature was tall but not straightened.
His movements were deliberate but not
hastened.
And though his heart was made of pure gold,
It was the very thing that would not allow him to
grow old.
His love was endless but very mild.
His demeanor cool, barely beyond the age of
child.
What he wouldn't give to achieve nobility.
What I wouldn't give to tell his story like a
trilogy.
But his life was narrowed down to a novel.
And now I write to stop from feeling awful.

Wholly

Merely an illusion, just a mess.
Slightly concave & quite depressed.
Simply a dream,
Solely a protest.
Purely a devil in a rose-colored dress.
Exclusively sanctioned,
Barely progressed.
Utterly lacking & never blessed.
Basically an answer,
Plainly a yes.
Totally wide open with only a guess.

Baseball

Man size appetite for a revolver
With bullets of blue & red lights.

Siblings in the doorway
With a wooden bat.

A mother & child
With a knife in hand.

One mile.
Just one mile.

Long red socks
And some bubblegum.

Safe.

Duncan MacDougall

"Duncan MacDougall believed the human soul
to weigh three/fourths of an ounce, twenty-one
grams, or about the weight of an adult human
big toe.

He tested six subjects who were living in an old
folks home dying of tuberculosis. He found that
four of the six subjects had lost some form of
body mass at the very second they died.

He later tested his theory again but on fifteen
dogs and found the results to be negative as none
of the subjects seemed to lose any body mass at
death."

Do souls grow like human toes?
Are souls the same size throughout life?
Or are they always equal to the size of our big
toe?
Do dogs even have souls?
Are souls only a human experience?
Or are we all losing something we'll never
understand?

Everlasting

Seeing you sad is something I want to mend.
Treasuring you like a jewel, loving you is never
to an extent.
So tell me you want everything you can't have
And I'll gladly spend the rest of my life
Parading around giving you the land.
Tell me you'll never want a sideways glance
And I'll make sure to praise what I can.
Cherish me while we're hand & hand
And I'll compliment the life you need.
Show me a romance that's everlasting
And I'll soak you in the nectar of Aphrodite.

Rapid Eye Movement

I touched him lightly just as I was about to sleep.
He murmured, "I love you."
My being resonates within his deep slumber.
I am his REM sleep.

Break Bread With Your Demons

I want to kiss you then tell you,
"You're too far-fetched for me."

I want to mellow your demons
As they leave your lips.

Tell them to break bread with me
In-between my hips.

I'd like to wine & dine them
Before attempting peace.

Watch them stop & squirm
Then all-together cease.

Mother Moon

My mother use to tell me that the craters of the
moon made the face of Jesus.
All I ever saw was a woman screaming for help.

To Sleep Or Die

I would wake up ready to sleep or die.
I desired substance.
I craved conversation.
I was receiving neither.
Right there was where I was suffocating the
most.
Between the nothing & the never.
I would curl up with my pain
And drown in my thoughts.
They had no titles
And when asked to describe them
I could not recount where they came from.
I could only stammer through complaints &
regrets.

Without You

I barred my bones in silver & gold
Then told myself you had no hold.
We sat below the cherry trees
Locking lips on bended knees.
I held my breath as you twisted your tongue.
A whistle blew & the angels sung.
Our vested summer was little but known.
I sat behind blue eyes as we made our way
home.
I kept my time pleasant & waiting
Never to notice you were gently fading.
Winter was calm unlike my heart.
We pushed pass the grim for our velvet start.
I was once so nimble, so sure.
Try as we might we had lost all allure.
Summer came & went,
Though it was time well spent,
I learned lust within someone new.
I had found love without you.

A Liar's Tale

I see shapes where there were once holes.
I see nudes within my skin without sores.
I resist the urge, a trade I took up to pass the
turn.
I should speak but instead I hide to feel the burn.
I have layers that don't candy coat much.
I have issues that cannot be touched.
I live life with little to do but thrive.
I tell lies, how else could I survive?

Double Take

He stares
At everyone else
But me
Just a little too long

And it's in that realization
That I go breathless.

Crush

You were hot air that I so badly wanted to be a
refreshing breeze.
You were the unneeded patriarch with beautiful
words that kept me tied in knots.
In a haste I threw it all away for in a day's time
you butchered my pipe-dream.
The exact same ideal that you planted in my
head
Wisdom & wounds were cultivated & molded.
Though my wishful thinking could be blamed,
It was you who shipped me abroad.
It was you that left me sinking.
Like a moth to a flame,
I was an addict, unashamed.

9 789358 369878